REVEREND FUN ... OFFLINE

BY DENNIS "MAX" HENGEVELD

GOSPEL COMMUNICATIONS
INTERNATIONAL INC®

P.O. Box 455 Muskegon, Michigan 49443
www.gospelcom.net

For current information about all releases from Gospel Communications International, visit our Web site: http://www.gospelcom.net/gci/

REVEREND FUN ... OFFLINE
By Dennis "Max" Hengeveld

Copyright © 2000 by Gospel Communications International
Published by Gospel Communications International
P.O. Box 455 Muskegon, MI 49443 (USA)

Library of Congress Cataloging-in-Publication Data
Hengeveld, Dennis ("Max")
     Reverend Fun ... Offline
     p. cm.
     Includes bibliographical references and indexes.
     ISBN 1-55568-183-2
     1. Humor (Christian) and family - United States
     2. Internet (Computer Network) and humor - United States
     I. Title
     II. Hengeveld, Dennis

Printed in the United States of America.

00   01   02   03   04   05   06   07   08   09   /   10   09   08   07   06   05   04   03   02   01

THIS BOOK IS DEDICATED TO MY DARLING WIFE, GAIL,
WHO LAUGHS AT ME MORE THAN ANYONE ELSE
YET DOES IT IN SUCH A CLEVER WAY
IT LETS ME THINK IT'S BECAUSE I AM ACTUALLY FUNNY

ACKNOWLEDGEMENTS

Reverend fun would not exist without Gospel Communications International.
GCI would not exist without the support of the many donors and contributors who
keep investing their time, energy, and resources into a project that is dear to them.
They have my gratitude, my respect, and probably a free copy of this book.

I would not be able to accomplish what I do at GCI without the contributions of the
awesome people with whom I work. I am fortunate to have a building full of spectacular
people who educate, encourage, and assist me in all that I do. I am lucky to have them.

I wouldn't be even close to where I am today if it wasn't for the unconditional love
and encouragement of my family and friends. They all have great amounts of
confidence in my abilities, and they are always right there to give me a boost and/or a hug
... which keeps me going.

I would also like to send a huge thanks to the many great readers of Reverend Fun who
have contributed their ideas, their suggestions, their criticisms, and their encouragement.
Without their support (and criticism) Reverend Fun wouldn't be as cool as it is today.

And, as always, thanks to God for the subject material!

USING REVEREND FUN IN YOUR PUBLICATION

HTTP://WWW.REVERENDFUN.COM/NEEDY/

You may reproduce the cartoons in this book, provided you follow a few simple guidelines: Proper attribution (© Gospel Communications International • Used by Permission), the website URL (www.reverendfun.com), and the title (Reverend Fun) must all be included with the cartoons you use. If you desire to use the cartoons in a publication or product that will be sold, visit the site to see if royalties are due. The site also has more information about getting and using cartoons.

Scan this (or copy it & cut it out) ....
and add it above cartoons you are using,
as seen in the example below

REVEREND FUN WWW.REVERENDFUN.COM

Scan this (or copy it & cut it out) ....
and add it to the right of the cartoons
you are using, as seen in the example below

©GOSPEL COMMUNICATIONS INTERNATIONAL · USED BY PERMISSION

Example use ....

REVEREND FUN WWW.REVERENDFUN.COM

©GOSPEL COMMUNICATIONS INTERNATIONAL · USED BY PERMISSION

CAPTION HERE

THANKS FOR TRAVELLING THOUSANDS OF MILES TO TEACH ME YOUR CHRISTIAN WAYS ... I'M OFF NOW AS A MISSIONARY TO AMERICA, I HEAR THERE IS A REAL NEED THERE

MAYBE YOU SHOULD TELL ME A LITTLE MORE ABOUT THIS GOD OF YOURS BEFORE WE GO ON

YES, I'M AWARE THAT OUR PROJECT DOESN'T MEET YOUR BUILDING CODE ... TELL YOU WHAT, JUST GIVE ME A WEEK

YES, IT SEEMS THAT YOUR FRIEND HERE IS COMPLETELY BONKERS; BUT THERE'S NOT REALLY MUCH WE CAN DO ABOUT IT ... YOU KNOW THAT WE CANNOT COMMIT AN ADULT TREE

MATTHEW 14:24-33

WELL, PETER, ALL YOU HAVE TO DO IS NOT TRUST IF YOU WANT TO GO BACK IN THE WATER

I HATE TO ASK YOU NICE FOLKS TO MOVE, BUT THE INN'S MARKET-ING DEPARTMENT FIGURES THAT IT WILL ONLY BE A MATTER OF TIME BEFORE THIS TREE GETS BETTER RECOGNITION THAN YOUR SON

I DON'T REALLY SEE MYSELF AS "UNSAVED", I PREFER TO CONSIDER MYSELF "ETERNITALLY CHALLENGED"

I THINK THAT YOU HAVE SOME SERIOUS FAITH ISSUES

I WAS GUNNA SHOOT YA TODAY, BUT I FOUND GOD ... NOW I SUSPECT WE SHOULD MEET AT DAWN AND HAVE A BIBLE VERSE MEMORY CONTEST INSTEAD

HEY, I THOUGHT I WAS IN CHARGE HERE ... WHO DIED AND MADE YOU BOSS?

GREAT TROUBLES WILL COME TO YOU AND YOUR PEOPLE: YOUR CROPS WILL PERISH, YOUR RIVERS WILL DRY UP, AND YOUR DESCENDANTS WILL ALL BE COMPUTER ILLITERATE

HOW MANY TIMES DO I HAVE TO TELL YOU? ... YOU'RE SUPPOSED TO LOVE YOUR NEIGHBOR AS YOURSELF

WAIT, COME BACK ... I SAID "YOU MUST BELIEVE" NOT "YOU MUST LEAVE BEE"

OOOOH THERE GO THOSE BLASTED "NON-FILLEDS" WITH THEIR "HOLIER-THAN-THOU" ATTITUDES

OK, YOU'VE NOW GOT LIGHT FOR "HEAVEN" AND THE "VOID" ... BUT WE WILL HAVE TO UPDATE THIS AFTER YOU CREATE "DRY LAND", "SKY" AND "SEAS"

ONCE AGAIN, DEVIL TED HAD TO EXPLAIN THAT THE TURKEY HAD BURNT BEFORE HE EVEN PUT IT IN THE OVEN

WE GIVE THANKS FOR ALL THE BOUNTY THAT FARMER BOB HAS BLESSED US ALL WITH THESE PAST FEW MONTHS

HERKIMER THE ANGEL KNEW THAT THIS WAS HEAVEN FOR SURE AS THE NEWSPAPER HAD NOTHING BUT GOOD NEWS TO REPORT

SORRY FELLA, CAN'T HELP YA ... YOU SHOULD REALLY MAKE A RESERVATION A FEW DAYS IN ADVANCE ... ESPECIALLY IF YOU KNOW THAT YOUR WHOLE NATION PLANS ON MOVING TOO

HOW MANY TIMES DO I HAVE TO TELL YOU, WE'RE ATTACKING HIVITES AND PERIZZITES, NOT HIVE-ITES AND PARASITES!

DEUTERONOMY 20:16-17

THE DEVIL MAKES WORK FOR IDOL HANDS

LET MY PEOPLE GO TO RECESS OR A GREAT PLAGUE SHALL FALL UPON THIS SCHOOL

IT'S A GOOD THING THAT YOU ARE AS WEE AS YOU ARE, ZACCHAEUS, BECAUSE WE FORGOT TO BRING THE SOCCER BALL

OH, "SPLIT THE RED SEA" ... I THOUGHT YOU SAID "SPLIT PEA"

LET HE WHO IS WITHOUT SIN CAST THE FIRST SNOW

I'M SORRY GUY, I KNOW THAT YOU'VE GOT A GOOD HEALTH PLAN AND YOU GIVE OUT FREE GIFTS AND ALL, BUT JESUS REALLY DOES HAVE A MUCH BETTER PLAN

WELL, MR. HEROD, AS YOUR NEW WISEMAN, I WOULD HAVE TO SAY THAT IF YOU NEED TO HIRE THREE WISEMEN TO FIND SOMETHING THAT IS MARKED BY A GIANT STAR, THEN PERHAPS YOU SHOULDN'T BE A KING AT ALL

I WAS SO EXCITED ABOUT THE BABY JESUS THAT I STARTED CLUCKING LIKE A FIEND ... AND THEN AN ANGEL OF THE LORD APPEARED BEFORE ME AND SAID UNTO ME ... "SHUT UP"

MY MOM MADE THIS FOR ME FOR THE CHRISTMAS PLAY AND NOW SHE IS SO PROUD OF IT THAT I AM NOT ALLOWED TO TAKE IT OFF

THIS YEAR, FOR NEW YEARS, I AM RESOLVING TO DO ALL SORTS OF BAD THINGS SINCE I NEVER EVER STICK TO MY NEW YEAR'S RESOLUTIONS

YOU THINK YOU'RE ALL THAT, WITH YOUR SLINGS AND YOUR STONES ... BUT I'VE GOT NEWS FOR YOU ... I'VE GOT SOME GOLIATH DNA AND WE'LL BE CLONING BEFORE YOU CAN SAY "TENS OF THOUSANDS"

I'M A DIFFERENT KIND OF ATHEIST ALTOGETHER

I'M REALLY PLEASED TO KNOW THAT YOU BOYS LIKE MY MESSAGE ... BUT I REALLY DON'T THINK THAT A MOSH PIT AND STAGE DIVING ARE NECESSARY

PASTOR'S SERMON IS GOING LONG AGAIN, ISN'T IT?

THE PASTOR WAS UPSET BECAUSE TOM ONLY PRETENDED TO LISTEN TO THE SERMONS ... SO NOW TOM DOESN'T PRETEND ANYMORE

HONESTLY, I THINK WE NEED MORE WOMEN PROPHETS ... THAT ELIJAH CHARACTER GAVE ME AN UNENDING SUPPLY OF OIL ... I NEEDED COOKING OIL AND HE GAVE ME 10W40

PETER'S EARLY ATTEMPTS TO WALK ON WATER WITH JESUS DISPLAYED AN INADEQUATE AMOUNT OF FAITH

LORD, IF I CAN JUST FIND TEN MEN IN THIS CITY WHO AREN'T DRESSED IN GRUNGE WILL YOU PLEASE SPARE US FROM ANY MORE ALTERNATIVE MUSIC

EVERYONE SAYS HOW PHONY THIS CHURCH IS, BUT I DON'T SEE HOW IT CAN BE BAD WHEN IT LOOKS SO NICE

WILL YOU BE MY VALENTINE?

GENESIS 4:1-15

OH CAIN, SO WHAT IF EVERYBODY IN CLASS LIKED MY ANIMAL CRACKERS BETTER THAN YOUR VEGETABLE CRACKERS

NO, TOM, THE RAPTURE IS NOT A MUSICAL EVENT

I HOPE YOU DON'T PLAN ON TRYING TO TELL ME THAT YOU WERE FIGHTING THE GOOD FIGHT AGAIN

LOOK PASTOR, NOW I CAN TELL YOU ABOUT SOME OF THE LEADERS AND HEROES FROM MY RELIGION

IT WAS SAID THAT IF IT WEREN'T FOR THE OFFERING-TAKING ABILITIES OF GOOD OL' SAD FRED, THE CHURCH WOULD'VE HAD TO SHUT DOWN YEARS AGO

I TOLD YOU THAT YOU FLY TOO FAST

MY DOG ATE MY SERMON

PASTOR ED ASSUMED THAT THE NEW PROJECTOR HAD JUST A LITTLE MORE POWER THAN WAS NEEDED

THIS IS GREAT, BUT IF I REMEMBER CORRECTLY, I ASKED FOR A ROOM WITH A PEW

I KNOW I'M SUPPOSED TO BE THE SHEPHERD OF THE FLOCK ... BUT I'M REALLY STARTING TO FEEL LIKE KEEPER OF THE ZOO

"HE WHO IS WITHOUT SIN CASTS THE FIRST STONE," RIGHT? WELL, I STILL HAVE THE FIRST STONE ... I THREW THE SECOND STONE AT HIM

YEAH DAD, WE KNOW THE DRILL ... FIRST YOU READ TO US ABOUT SHADRACH, THEN YOU READ TO US ABOUT MESHACH AND THEN TO BED WE GO

SOOO, AARON ... YOU ACTUALLY EXPECT ME TO BELIEVE THAT YOU "ACCIDENTALLY" DROPPED A BUNCH OF GOLD IN THE FIRE AND IT JUST "HAPPENED" TO COME OUT LOOKING LIKE THIS CALF HERE?!?

WHERE HAVE YOU BEEN ADAM? AND WHY ARE YOU ON CRUTCHES? AND WHO ARE ALL THESE WOMEN? AND WHY IS YOUR CHEST ALL CAVED IN AND HOLLOW-LOOKING LIKE THAT?

I AM RUNNING A CHRISTIAN OPERATING SYSTEM CALLED "STAINED GLASS WINDOWS 2000" ... IT'S PRETTY COOL BECAUSE WHEN YOU MAKE AN ERROR THE COMPUTER SAYS "FORGIVE THEM FATHER FOR THEY KNOW NOT WHAT THEY DO"

IT WAS A WHILE BEFORE THE PENGUIN CHURCH MEMBERS WERE ABLE TO ACCEPT THIS STRANGE AND IRREVERENT LOOKING STRANGER

IF WE BELIEVE IN THE TRINITY, THEN SHOULDN'T WE BE CALLED "GODTIANS" AND NOT JUST "CHRISTIANS"?

YOUR CAESAR SALAD SIR

A BAD TIME TO BE A CHERUB

THIS WORKS SO MUCH BETTER THAN OL' ROVER DID

SURE MY NEW CAR IS REALLY THIN, BUT I DON'T CARE BECAUSE I PLAN TO TRAVEL THE STRAIGHT AND NARROW

I DON'T KNOW WHY THE SONG SAID TO TELL THIS TO THE MOUNTAIN, BUT HERE GOES, "JESUS CHRIST IS BORN"

THE SERPENT'S EARLIER ATTEMPT TO TEMPT EVE REMAINED FRUITLESS

2 KINGS 2:1-11

I TOLD YOU I WOULD PRAY FOR YOU ... NOT PAY FOR YOU

I HAVEN'T EVEN TURNED MY COMPUTER ON SINCE OUR NEW CHRISTIAN BOSS TOLD US THAT WE WILL BE JUDGED BY OUR FAITH AND NOT BY OUR WORKS

JOE THE DEVIL HATED THIS NEW "SCARED STRAIGHT" PROGRAM

YOUR ROBO-PASTOR ISN'T DEFECTIVE AFTER ALL ... IT JUST SEEMS THAT SOMEBODY PUT IT ON ITS "YOUTH PASTOR" SETTING WHICH TRIGGERS A "TEENAGER IDENTIFICATION" PROGRAM

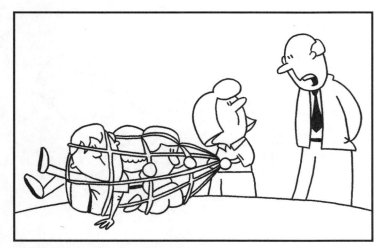

I DON'T CARE WHAT YOUR SISTER TOLD YOU, THIS IS NOT WHAT I MEANT BY "FISHER OF MEN"

I THINK THAT WE PRAY MORE ON SUNDAY BECAUSE THE RATES ARE CHEAPER

DON'T YOU EVER WISH THAT WE WERE FISHERS OF WOMEN INSTEAD?

SO, JESUS, HAVE YOU MADE ANY PLANS FOR EASTER YET?

SLUGGO AND I ARE TAKIN' AN OFFERIN' THAT YOUZ JUST CAN'T REFUSE

SAY, DO YOU THINK YOU COULD BE A GOOD GUARD AND FETCH US SOME MORE MARSHMALLOWS? ... SHADRACH KEEPS EATING THEM ALL BEFORE WE CAN FINISH PUTTING OUR SMORES TOGETHER

JESUS LOVES EVE N' ME

SORRY WE DIDN'T COME FORWARD AT YOUR HALFTIME SERMON, PASTOR BOB ... WE'RE NOT REALLY THE KIND OF PEOPLE TO MAKE A STAND LIKE THAT IN PUBLIC

OH, LOOK AT YOU WITH YOUR STAFF, AND YOUR CLOAK, AND YOUR BEARD ... THAT WHOLE LOOK IS JUST SOOOOOO B.C.

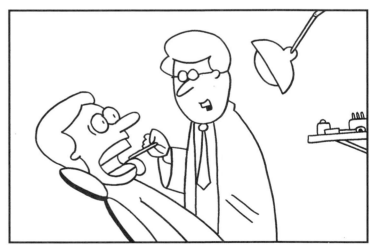

HMMMM ... KIND OF IRONIC THAT I HEARD YOU SINGING "CROWN HIM WITH MANY CROWNS" EARLIER

JOE FINALLY DECIDED TO SURRENDER HIS HEART TO GOD

TODAY IN SUNDAY SCHOOL WE LEARNED ABOUT "GLADLY", THE CROSS-EYED BEAR

IT'S MY NEW "TICKLE-ME-ELMIAS" DOLL ... HE LAUGHS IN BOTH HEBREW AND IN ENGLISH

I'M SORRY ERIC, BUT THE HUMAN BODY CAN ONLY SUPPORT SO MANY WITNESS PINS

PARTY OF TWO FOR TITHING OR NON-TITHING TODAY?

DON'T YOU THINK THAT YOU ARE TAKING THIS "HIGH PRIEST" GIG JUST A LITTLE TOO FAR?

AT THE FIRST SUPPER

RING THE BOTTLE
HALO TOSS

AND ONCE AGAIN MOSES' TEAM WON THE TOURNAMENT

WHY CAN'T YOU JUST BE LIKE THAT JESUS BOY IN YOUR CLASS ...
HE ALWAYS BEHAVES AND HAS HIS HOMEWORK DONE ON TIME

THERE IT IS ... THAT UFO I WAS TELLING YOU ABOUT

IN THE ANGEL COMMAND CENTER

EXODUS 16

ON HOT N' SPICY MANNA DAY

THE DOWNSIDE TO WALKING ON WATER

KINDA FUNNY HEY ... ME WORKING FOR YOU

IT'S TRUE, MY DOUBLE EDGED SWORD IS EXTREMELY DANGEROUS, BUT I ONLY USE IT FOR CUTTING DOUBLE-SIDED TAPE

NUMBERS 22:22-34

NO, I'M SORRY, BALAAM IS NOT IN AT THE MOMENT ... MAY I TAKE A MESSAGE?

LOOK EVE, I PICKED YOU A NICE NEW OUTFIT

DON'T YOU JUST LOVE NEW RECRUITS

OH ADAM, DID YOU GO AND MIX THE LIGHT AND DARK LEAVES AGAIN?

YES, YOU ARE SUPPOSED TO HONOR YOUR FATHER AND MOTHER, BUT THIS SHRINE IS TAKING IT A LITTLE BIT TOO FAR

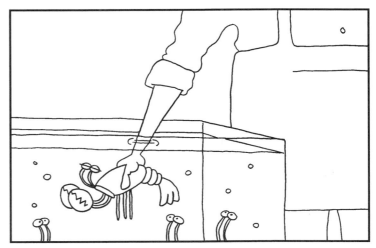

DEAR LORD, PLEASE BLESS THIS FOOD FOR WHICH THEY ARE ABOUT TO PARTAKE ... PLEASE BLESS IT NOW, PLEASE BLESS IT RIGHT NOW

SO YOU WANT TO HAVE YOUR BOOK OF "TED" CANONIZED, HUH?
WELL WHAT KIND OF NAME IS "TED"? AND WHERE IS YOUR BEARD?
AND HOW DO WE KNOW THIS PASSAGE OF YOURS IS "GOD
BREATHED" AND NOT "TED BREATHED"? HMMMMMMMM?

TRY AS HE MAY, ANGEL BOB JUST COULDN'T MUSTER UP AN EVIL EYE

THE PAPERBOY WAS JUST ONE OF MANY WHO FAILED TO UNDERSTAND
TOM'S INTENSE FEAR OF FAILING TO ENTERTAIN ANGELS UNAWARES

IN THE NAME OF JESUS ... COME OUT!!!

I DON'T CARE HOW GOOD YOU ALL FEEL ... I HATE CHANGE

AFTER JUST STRUGGLING TO PICK NAMES FOR THE PLATYPUS, THE AUK, THE RHINOCEROS AND THE GIBBON, ADAM WAS NOT IN THE MOOD TO WASTE MUCH THOUGHT ON THIS "EATER OF ANTS"

IN SPIRITUAL WARFARE YOU NEED A SPIRIT-GUN, LIKE THIS ONE

MAYBE WE WOULDN'T STILL BE WANDERING IN THE DESERT IF YOU HAD JUST TRADED IN THIS JUNKY OL' CAMEL-WAGON

OK, DELILAH, THE SECRET OF MY STRENGTH LIES IN MY MODEM ... REPLACE MY HIGH BANDWIDTH WITH A 28.8 AND I WILL BE HELPLESS

SORRY I HAD TO SPLIT THE SEA LIKE THAT, BUT THOSE BLASTED EGYPTIANS WERE GETTIN' PRETTY CLOSE

GIVE IT UP WITH THAT STUPID SIGN ALREADY AND COME CHECK OUT THIS AWESOME STAR THAT WE SPOTTED OVER BETHLEHEM

IF WE ARE BORN AGAIN, THEN HOW COME WE ONLY HAVE ONE BELLYBUTTON?

THE OLD "HALO GAG"

LATER MOSES AGAIN IMPRESSED THE PHARAOH'S MAGIC MEN WITH A GAG CAN OF EXPLODING SNAKES

OK, OK, ENOUGH ... YOU'VE MADE YOUR POINT ALREADY

BUZZ OFF, CREEP ... DON'T YOU HAVE A PLAGUE TO GO TO?

WHEN PUNISHMENT WAS NECESSARY BUT NO STONES WERE HANDY

OH, I AIN'T IN MOURNIN' DUDE ... SACKCLOTH IS IN STYLE

AN EXAMPLE OF A CARDINAL SIN

I STILL DON'T GET WHY JOSHUA WON'T LET ME HAVE A SOLO

ONCE I WAS BLIND, BUT NOW I CAN SEE

YOUR IDEAS ARE INTRIGUING ... PLEASE ENLIGHTEN US

46

NUMBERS 22:22-34

YO, BALAAM, US ANIMALS WERE JUST WONDERING WHY YOU DON'T GET FREAKED OUT WHEN ANIMALS TALK TO YOU

I'M AFRAID I DON'T HAVE ANYTHING IN THE WAY OF A LAND OF MILK AND HONEY, BUT YOU LOOK LIKE MEN OF GOD ... I CAN GET YOU A DEAL ON A LAND OF MILK AND EGGS

WHEN I AM DOING SOMETHING NAUGHTY, I TELL PEOPLE THAT THIS BRACELET MEANS "WHAT WOULDN'T JESUS DO?" SO THAT THEY DON'T THINK THAT I AM A HYPOCRITE

FIRST THORNS, THEN PAINFUL CHILDBIRTH, AND NOW THESE
INCESSANT PHONE CALLS ASKING US TO SWITCH OUR LONG
DISTANCE CARRIERS

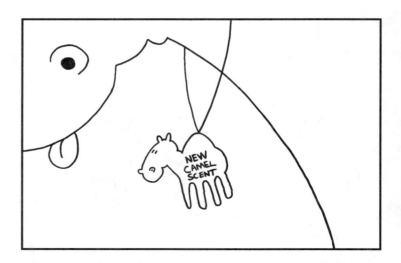

SQUAWK ... YOU MUST BE BORN AGAIN

WHEN YOU WERE GONE YESTERDAY I GOT HER TO PLAY SOME
HEAVY METAL

YOU SAID WWW.TENCOMMANDMENTS.COM CORRECT?

NEBUCHADNEZZAR AT THE RUNNING OF THE BULLS

WALLY'S ATTITUDE OF "IF YOU CAN'T BEAT 'EM, JOIN 'EM" CAME IN REALLY HANDY DURING THE LOCUST PLAGUE

OH SILLY ME, I CREATED A ONE-OF-A-KIND WEBSITE, DID ALL THE NECESSARY PROMOTION BUT FORGOT TO DO THE DEMOGRAPHICS

HAVING LOST THE RECIPE, DON TRIED TO MAKE AN ANGEL FOOD CAKE FROM MEMORY

O SPLENDID, IT LOOKS LIKE THEY LET MILDRED DO THE BULLETINS AGAIN

DO WE HAVE TO GIVE BACK THE COED NAKED GARDENING T-SHIRTS?

O WAIT, THERE'S SOME EVEN FUNNIER STUFF IN CHAPTER TWO

HEY WARDEN, I'M IN CHARGE OF THE PRISON BIBLE STUDY THIS WEEK AND MY TOPIC IS "YOU REAP WHAT YOU SOW" ... I'M GOING TO NEED A FEW SHOVELS FOR THIS OF COURSE, AND MAYBE A HOE ... AND PROBABLY A LADDER

TEACHERS ALWAYS PULL THE OL' "HEZEKIAH GAG" WHENEVER WE DO THESE SPEED DRILLS, SO I HAD THIS SPECIAL BIBLE MADE UP WITH AN EXTRA CHAPTER NAMED "HEZEKIAH" ... I CAN'T WAIT TO SEE HOW THIS GOES OVER

IT WASN'T UNTIL LATER THAT NOAH EXPLAINED THE "SNIPE OVERBOARD" GAG TO A NOT-VERY-HAPPY CREW

PLEASE INSERT YOUR CREDIT CARD TO BEGIN YOUR ELECTRONIC OFFERING TRANSACTION

IF YOU DON'T MIND ... I WAS TALKING TO THAT BUSH

THE LORD IS MY SHEPHERD, I SHALL NOT BE IN WANT. HE MAKES ME LIE DOWN IN GREEN PASTURES ...

SUDDENLY TED DISCOVERED THAT HE WAS STANDING IN THE MIDST OF A SUNDAY SCHOOL OF FISH

I REALLY APPRECIATE ALL THAT YOU DO FOR ME, MR. GOODNESS AND MR. MERCY, BUT I GOT THIS RESTRAINING ORDER BECAUSE THE THOUGHT OF YOU TWO FOLLOWING ME ALL THE REST OF MY DAYS KINDA CREEPS ME OUT

I'M DREADFULLY SORRY ABOUT THAT ... IT'S JUST THAT BILL WAS REALLY MOVED DURING LAST WEEK'S "THE SEVENTH DAY IS THE DAY OF REST" SERMON

CAN'T WAIT FOR GLORY ... THEY WILL FINALLY CLAP TOGETHER ON THE OFF-BEAT!

LUKE 6:31

OH YOU'RE QUITE WELCOME FOR THE BIRTHDAY PICNIC FELLA ... I'M JUST DOIN' FER MY NEIGHBOR AS I'D HAVE MY NEIGHBOR DO FER ME ... OH, AND BY THE WAY, I REALLY LIKE T-BONE

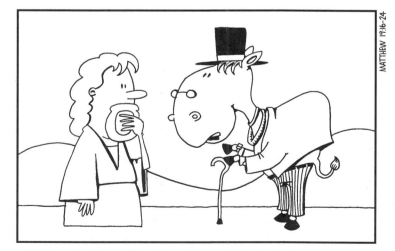

MATTHEW 19:16-24

SO TELL ME THEN, JESUS, HOW HARD WOULD IT BE FOR A RICH CAMEL TO ENTER THE KINGDOM OF HEAVEN

55

HEY, GOD, IT'S CAIN ... MY SACRIFICE IS STILL VEGETABLES ... BUT NOW I'VE CLEVERLY SHAPED THEM LIKE AN ANIMAL

AM I A DOG, THAT YOU COME AT ME WITH STICKS?

YOU'RE PLANNING ON BEING HERE A WHILE, AREN'T YOU?

OOH LOOKEE I GOT A PAGE ... IT'S FROM GOD ... IT SAYS "YOU CAN'T HIDE FROM ME GUYS, ESPECIALLY WITH YOUR PAGER SET TO BEEP MODE"

REALLY NOAH, WE'LL BE FINE

JOB, JOB, I WAS IN THE I.T. DEPARTMENT WHEN ALL OF OUR SERVER HARD DRIVES MELTED DOWN AND I AM THE ONLY ONE WHO HAS ESCAPED TO TELL YOU

I'M SURE THAT YOU ARE SURPRISED, MR. ELIJAH, BUT DO YOU REALLY THINK THAT THIS IS WHAT I EXPECTED WHEN I STARTED WORKING AT RAVEN PIZZA?

JUST LOOK AT THIS COLOR, IT JUST WON'T GO WITH MY SKIRT ... OH ADAM, I DON'T HAVE A THING TO WEAR

WHENEVER I GO ON ONE OF MY CALLINGS I BRING "PROPHET-AID" ANTI-SKEPTIC LOTION ... TRY SOME, IT WILL MAKE A BELIEVER OUT OF YOU

YOU INVESTED A FEMALE AND A MALE SHEEP WITH US, SOON AFTER THOUGH, A BEAR MARKET ATE HALF OF YOUR ASSETS ... BUT THE REMAINING SHEEP HAS SINCE SPLIT AND NOW YOUR LIVE STOCK IS GROWING DRAMATICALLY

2 KINGS 2:11

CHARIOTS OF FIRE WERE QUITE POPULAR AT CAMPGROUNDS

MATTHEW 14:14-21

YOU ALL DID A GREAT JOB FEEDING THE 5000 ... BUT NOW I NEED YOU TO SEE IF YOU CAN FIND A LAD IN THE CROWD WHO HAS A BREATH MINT

OH PETER GO BACK TO LAND ... YOU KNOW PERFECTLY WELL THAT I DON'T HAVE ANY GREY POUPON

DUE TO NEW LOCAL FIRE CODES, WE ARE NO LONGER ALLOWED TO CONSIDER OURSELVES "ON FIRE FOR CHRIST"

VERILY, VERILY, VERILY, VERILY I SAY UNTO YOU ... LIFE IS BUT A DREAM

OH JONAH, PLEASE DON'T TELL ME THAT YOU'RE GOING TO WEAR THAT T-SHIRT ALL DAY AT THE BEACH AGAIN

WHAT DO YOU MEAN, "NOT THAT KIND OF ARC"?

THE CONTROVERSIAL STEALTH ANGEL

WOULD YOU PLEASE WATCH OVER MY LAST SHEEP MISTER?
... THAT BLASTED WOLF HAS STOLEN ALL MY OTHERS

LISTEN TO ME, FAITHFUL WORSHIPPER, I WANT YOU TO GO AND
WORSHIP THIS GOD OF THE ISRAELITES ... HE IS COOL, I AM
WORTHLESS AND UGLY

HAH HAH, YOU JUST TOLD HIM THAT HE HAS A SPLINTER IN HIS EYE,
AND YOU HAVE A BEAM IN YOURS

THE BOARD DECIDED THAT JOHN WILL REMAIN THE HEAD GREETER ... AT LEAST UNTIL HIS MEDICATION WEARS OFF

SHEPHERD HUMOR

I'M MAKING A SPECIAL EXCEPTION FOR YOU AND I DON'T WANT YOU TO GO BLABBING TO ANYONE I MIGHT BAPTIZE LATER

ELEMENTARY MATHEMATICS CAIN, IF YOU HAVE NO APPLES, AND I GIVE YOU AN APPLE, THEN YOU HAVE ONE APPLE ... IF EVE GIVES IT TO YOU, THEN YOU END UP WITH NOTHING

DON'T GET TOO EXCITED, FELLA, I'M THE MEDIOCRE SAMARITAN ... I ONLY GIVE YOU A BANDAID AND THEN I'M OFF

C'MON, GUYS, STOP GIVING ME JIVE ... YOU KNOW PERFECTLY WELL THAT IT WAS THE DEVIL DRESSED UP LIKE A SNAKE

THE BAD SHEPHERD DOES CARE FOR HIS SHEEP, BUT IS ALWAYS PULLING SOME SORT OF PRANK ON THEM

NOT A WORD ... I'M HAVING IT CLEANED NEXT WEEK

WE'RE PLAYING FOLLOW THE LEADER AND YOU'RE THE PASTOR SO I GUESS YOU GOT THE JOB

MATTHEW 28:19

WELL, WE FINALLY BROUGHT THE GOSPEL TO A PLACE IT HAS NEVER BEEN ... BUT WE SHOULD'VE CHECKED TO SEE IF THERE WERE PEOPLE HERE FIRST

EXODUS 20:1-21

SORRY PAL, I KNOW THAT "THOU SHALT NOT STEAL" PART IS REALLY GOING TO HURT YOUR BUSINESS ... I'M HAVING A HARD TIME DEALING WITH THE "KILL" PART MYSELF

IT'S OUR "BEST OF BULLETINS" COLLECTION

I CAN'T SAY FOR SURE, BUT IN THIS CASE I THINK THAT GOD MIGHT ACTUALLY NOT PREFER THE FATTED CALF

YOU CAN ALWAYS TELL HOW FANCY THE RESTAURANT IS BY HOW WELL THEY PRESENT THE LOCUST

OH SURE, YOU MAY HAVE HEARD BAD THINGS ABOUT THE WAY OUR CHURCH RECRUITS NEW MEMBERS, BUT IF YOU JUST STICK AROUND FOR A LITTLE LONGER I AM SURE YOU WILL BE ABLE TO MAKE UP YOUR MIND FOR YOURSELF

GENESIS 6-8

JACK THE FALSE PROPHET'S "DOG RESURRECTION" SCHEME ONLY SUCCEEDED IN GETTING HIM FREELANCE TAXIDERMY WORK

Y'KNOW ... I JUST DON'T THINK I BELIEVE IN ATHEISTS

THIS WAS THE BIG MOMENT, THE PART OF THE SPEECH THAT HAD BEEN MESSED UP REPEATEDLY IN PRACTICE, AND THE TENSION WAS HIGH

WILL THAT BE SMOKING OR NON?

BEFORE A SHEPHERD CAN ACHIEVE "GOOD SHEPHERD" STATUS HE MUST FIRST ATTEND A SHEEP AWARENESS SEMINAR

THIS ALWAYS HAPPENS WHEN THE FRIED CHICKEN JOINT NEXT DOOR HAS THEIR BIG SUNDAY SPECIALS

I KNOW YOU ASKED ME TO "COME FOURTH" ... BUT I TRIPPED

THIS BABY IS PACKIN' A TOTAL OF TWO OXEN POWER

THE NUMBER OF SUCCESSFUL MIRACLES HAS DROPPED REGARDLESS OF THE COMMITTEES, TASK FORCES AND FOCUS GROUPS THAT WE HAVE BEEN SERVING ON RECENTLY

REMEMBER THE PLAN ... JUST RUN OUT THERE, OPEN YOUR JACKET AND TELL THOSE GUYS THAT IF THEY DON'T CONVERT RIGHT NOW YOU'RE GUNNA START A WHOLE NEW UNIVERSE

OH STOP YOUR POUTING ... YOU WERE THERE WHEN NOAH WARNED US WOODPECKERS

OK, THAT'S THREE NOW, GOD ... I THINK THAT I'VE PROVED THAT I WON'T CURSE BY NOW ... DO YOU THINK THAT YOU CAN MAYBE LET ME CATCH THE NEXT ONE?

I RAN INTO THE STORE FOR JUST A MINUTE AND WHEN I CAME OUT I COULDN'T FIND SHEEP NUMBER FORTY-TWO

I'M IMPRESSED WITH YOUR TIME MANAGEMENT SKILLS, RANDY, BUT I JUST DON'T THINK YOU SHOULD COMBINE SPEEDWALKING WITH THE OFFERING ANYMORE

GENESIS 11:1-9

AFTER THE TOWER OF BABEL INCIDENT

WHILE I WAS PRAYING FOR SAFETY THIS THANKSGIVING THIS WORM FELL OFF OF MY BEAK ... AND HERE I HAD BEEN THINKING THAT I HAD A WATTLE

SHE STARTED IT

DON'T WORRY, I ONLY DO THIS DURING CHOIR TRYOUTS

WE'VE HAD A RUN OF PRETTY BAD LUCK LATELY, EVE, BUT I HAVE A PRETTY GOOD FEELING ABOUT THIS 'WORK' THING

LOOKING PATHETIC IS ONLY GOING TO MAKE THINGS WORSE FOR YOU ... US LIONS LIKE TO PRAY ON THE SICK AND WEAK

AND YOU SAID THAT GOOD FISHERMEN DON'T WEAR TIES

YES, EVEN TURKEYS HAVE SOMETHING TO BE THANKFUL FOR ON THANKSGIVING ... PERSONALLY, I'M THANKFUL THAT I LOST SO MUCH WEIGHT WHEN I WAS SICK LAST MONTH

OH SURE, FIVE MINUTES AGO YOU'RE STEALING MY HORSE, BUT WHEN I TELL YOU TO SAY YOUR PRAYERS YOU SUDDENLY FIND RELIGION

OH DON'T WORRY ABOUT RUSTY, HE'S TRAINED TO SNIFF OUT NON-CHRISTIANS ... SAY, MAYBE YOU'D LIKE TO COME TO OUR BIBLE STUDY TONIGHT

MISSY USED TO BE A STEWARDESS

ALTHOUGH KEVIN'S EXPERIMENTS WITH LEADING GOATS TO THE SLAUGHTER PROVIDED SOME INTERESTING RESULTS, THEY WERE WIDELY IGNORED DUE TO A LACK OF PLACEBOS AND CONTROL GOATS

YOU WIN THIS TIME, BUT THERE WILL COME A DAY WHEN YOU CAN'T AFFORD A RENT-A-COP ANYMORE, AND I'LL BE THERE

HEY, THANKS FOR HANGING ON TO MY PRESCRIPTIONS AND FOR PUTTING MY MONEY IN THE OFFERING WHILE I CLEANED MY PURSE

OH I WOULDN'T WORRY ABOUT GETTING LOST ... WISEMAN #1 TOLD ME THAT HE HAS SOME SORT OF GLOBAL POSITIONING SYSTEM

OH, LOOKIT THAT ... NOAH'S INVITE HAS AN RSVP

STOP TALKING SILLY GUYS, YOU KNOW THAT WE HAD IT WAY WORSE IN THE MALL OF EGYPT ... TRUST MOSES, HE WILL FIND US A WAY OUT OF HERE

HELP ME OUT HERE, WHAT'S MY MOTIVATION? ... I NEED TO FIND THE CENTER OF THIS "INNKEEPER" CHARACTER AND WHAT MOVES HIM

HOW ABOUT IF, INSTEAD OF GIVING YOU EVERYTHING THAT YOU THINK YOU WANT FOR CHRISTMAS, I GIVE YOU WHAT YOU NEED?

WELL WHAT DO YOU KNOW, YOU'RE RIGHT, IT DOESN'T SAY "DO UNTO OTHERS AS YOU'VE HAD THEM DO UNTO YOU"

I'M ACTUALLY SECOND PETER, THIS IS FIRST PETER TO MY RIGHT AND THIRD PETER IS ON FIRST PETER'S RIGHT ... YOU'LL HAVE TO FORGIVE US AS WE ARE OUT OF ORDER AGAIN

MY OTHER CHARIOT IS A BMW

I KNOW YOU WANT TO FIT IN AND BE "ALTERNATIVE" ... BUT THIS NEW THING WITH WEARING YOUR WAISTCLOTH DOWN LOW LIKE THAT IS TOO MUCH

HEY GOD ... WHICH CAME FIRST?

I GUESS NOW WOULD BE A GOOD TIME TO REMIND YOU ALL ABOUT THE SPECIAL OFFERING WE ARE TAKING TODAY FOR A NEW PULPIT

AHHHHHHHHHH ... LOOK OUT, IT'S A PLAGUE OF HUMANS

O YEAH ... WE'RE FASTING THIS WEEK

JONAH REALIZED TWO THINGS THAT DAY ... YOU CAN'T ESCAPE GOD'S WILL, AND THAT IF HE HAD SHOWERED LAST WEEK HE MIGHT HAVE BEEN IN THE WHALE FOR A WHILE LONGER

I DON'T UNDERSTAND WHY ALL OF US ANIMALS HAVE TO GO TOO ... SHOOT, I DON'T EVEN LIKE APPLES

YOUNG JOSHUA AT THE SNOWBALL BATTLE OF JERICHO

ONE TIME I WAS PRAYING REALLY INTENTLY FOR A LONG LIFE, BUT I WASN'T PAYING ENOUGH ATTENTION AND I ENDED UP SAYING "WIFE" BY ACCIDENT

EXODUS 20:8

I WAS HOPING TO KEEP THE SABBATH DAY HOLY, BUT I CAN'T EVEN FIND IT ON THE CALENDAR

TIM THE SHEPHERD WAS SO THANKFUL FOR HIS NEW SHEEP THAT HE INSTANTLY WENT TO THE CHURCH TO GIVE TEN PERCENT BACK TO GOD

WELL WHAT HAVE WE HERE? LOOKS LIKE AN ARTIFICIAL ARM WITH A MISSING FINGER AND AN "I CAN'T BELIEVE IT'S NOT A SACKCLOTH" GARMENT ... YEAH IT'S A CON JOB ALRIGHT

AHA ... I CAUGHT YOU RED HANDED ... WHY DON'T YOU JUST STOP FOLDING THAT BILL AND BACK AWAY FROM THE COLLECTION PLATE

THIS CHURCH GET-AWAY WAS A GREAT IDEA, BUT IF I HEAR ONE MORE PERSON SAY "FORGIVE ME FATHER, FOR I HAVE SAND", I'M LEAVING

I THESSELONIANS 4:16

GRACE CEMETERY

POST-RAPTURE SALE
GOING ON NOW !!
MANY NEW OPENINGS

BARBER BOB PROVED TO BE ONE OF THE MOST DIFFICULT CHALLENGERS TO SAMSON

HONESTLY ADAM, IF YOU CRACK ONE MORE JOKE ABOUT ME "RAISING CAIN" I'M GOING TO INVENT THE DOGHOUSE THIS VERY INSTANT AND YOU'LL BE SLEEPING IN IT TONIGHT

SORRY FELLA, WE'RE NOT SERVING COFFEE TODAY

I KNOW YOU LOVE THE DOG, JESUS, BUT YOU'VE JUST GOTTA STOP RESURRECTING HIM LIKE THAT

HMMMM ... YOU'VE BEEN GNASHING YOUR TEETH AGAIN, HAVEN'T YOU

IT'S BEEN DOING THIS EVER SINCE I GOT CONFUSED AND PUT A BOTTLE OF ANTICHRIST IN MY RADIATOR

WE SORTA HAD SOMETHING DIFFERENT IN MIND, ADAM

86

AS HEAD ANGEL IN CHARGE OF COUNTING THE HAIRS OF HEADS, I WOULD LIKE TO PRESENT YOU WITH THIS AWARD FOR MAKING MY JOB SO EASY

"VERILY", THOUGHT MOSES, "THESE GENERIC DEODORANTS ARE NOT TO BE TRUSTED"

DEAR GOD, IF YOU LET ME MAKE THIS FOUL SHOT I PROMISE TO STOP SKIPPING CHURCH TO PLAY BALL

WHENEVER I PUT A PRAYER REQUEST ON OUR CHURCH WEBSITE IT GOES TO THE BOTTOM OF THE LIST ... LOOK HERE, I PUT IN THIS ONE WHEN MY GERBIL GOT SICK

YOU'VE BEEN DOING A GREAT JOB SERVING OTHERS, BUT YOU GOTTA STOP ASKING FOR TIPS

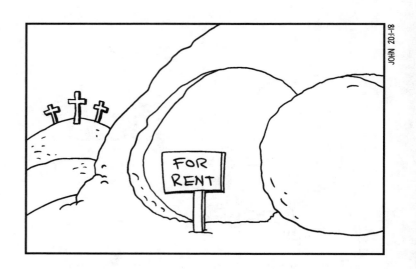

JOHN 20:1-18

I'M HERE AS **YOUR** GUARDIAN ANGEL

2 CORINTHIANS 10:5

I AM TAKING MY THOUGHTS CAPTIVE

WOW ... THAT WAS THE BEST SERMON ON TITHING THAT I HAVE EVER BEEN TO

I'VE BEEN DEBUGGING YOUR CREATION MODEL AND, NATURALLY, THERE WERE NO ERRORS ... WHEN I ADD THE SIN VARIABLE, HOWEVER, THINGS GET NASTY

STOP FEELING SORRY FOR YOURSELF ... YOU'RE NOT THE FIRST ONE WHO THOUGHT HE COULD BLOW OUT THE PILOT LIGHT Y'KNOW

JOSEPH, COME QUICK ... JESUS IS TAKING HIS FIRST STEPS

LUKE 19:1-10

WELL HELLO FELLA, YOU MUST BE THE LITTLE ACROPHOBIC BROTHER
I'VE BEEN HEARING SO MUCH ABOUT

GENESIS 6-8

HEY NOAH ... JOEL'S BEEN SAYING THAT THE ARK IS A CRAZY IDEA,
BUT ME AND MY WIFE BELIEVE YOU ... TAKE US, TAKE US

GENESIS 6-8

YOU GOTTA SEE THIS NOAH ... WE TAUGHT THE MOCKINGBIRD TO
MOCK A HAWK AND THEN THREW HIM IN THE RODENT ROOM

YOUR FATHER HAS AGREED TO STAY AWAKE IN CHURCH TODAY SINCE IT IS MOTHER'S DAY ... IT WOULD BE NICE IF YOU WOULD DO THE OPPOSITE FOR ONCE

EXODUS 19:18-20

HELLO GOOD SIR, ARE YOU ON YOUR WAY TO SPEAK WITH GOD? MAYBE YOU WOULD BE INTERESTED IN SOME "GLORY BLOCKER" SUNGLASSES ... IT GETS PRETTY BRIGHT UP THERE

WELL, I DON'T REALLY SNEEZE THAT OFTEN ... BUT IF I DO, I SUPPOSE YOU DON'T NEED TO SAY "GOD BLESS YOU"

EXODUS 7-12

EXCUSE ME WAITER ... THERE'S A FLY IN MY SOUP... AND IN MY BEVERAGE ... AND IN MY HAIR

LESSON LEARNED ... NEVER TRUST A TALKING SNAKE

HELLO MRS. GUSTAFSON, GUESS WHAT ... THIS IS THE FIRST ALTAR CALL I'VE MADE ON THE NEW CHURCH TELEPHONE

EXODUS 7-12

AND THE PHARAOH HARDENED HIS HEART ONCE AGAIN DURING THE PLAGUE OF FLIES

WELL WELL ... SPEAK OF THE DEVIL

CONGRATULATIONS SIR ... YOU JUST WON THE "MOST HUMBLE PASTOR" AWARD

ARRRR ... THIS IS WHERE ME TREASURE IS, NOW WHERE DID I PUT ME HEART?

WHEN MOSES GOT HELD UP AT THE LOCAL WATERING HOLE

GOTCHA!!! ... SIMON DIDN'T SAY "YOU MAY BE SEATED"

I'VE DECIDED TO REMEMBER THE SABBATH DAY AND KEEP IT HOLY SEVEN DAYS A WEEK

NATE'S CALL TO THE MISSION FIELD WASN'T QUITE AS STRONG AS HIS LOYALTY TO HIS LOCAL NEIGHBORHOOD

HEY, PASTOR, LAST WEEK'S "MORE LIKE JESUS" SERMON REALLY INSPIRED ME

FEAR NOT LITTLE ONE, I AM ACTUALLY A BIRD OF "PRAY"

UMM JESUS ... WE WERE GOING TO SKIP SOME ROCKS AT THE POND BUT IT SEEMS YOU ARE THE ONLY ONE WHO CAN CAST THE FIRST STONE

MATTHEW 14:24-33

ONCE PETER'S FAITH WAS SECURE, HE AND JESUS WERE A CINCH IN THE TWO-MAN SYNCHRONIZED SWIMMING EVENT

THE END OF THE WORLD IS NEAR

JUST ANOTHER BEAR WE HAVE TO CROSS

I SAMUEL 17

BORK

HEY, YOU NUTTY ISRAELITES LUCKED OUT AGAINST GOLIATH, BUT WOULD YOU DARE TO TRY YOUR LUCK AGAINST OUR NEXT BEST WARRIOR, IGOR?

I THINK THAT I'LL CALL YOU CHICKEN ... NO WAIT!!! ... MAYBE FRIED CHICKEN ... OR HOT N' SPICY CHICKEN ... MMMMM SPICY

STOP YOUR SULKING MAN ... YOU KNOW PERFECTLY WELL WHY EVERYONE ALWAYS BLAMES YOU FOR EVERYTHING

TODAY'S SERMON ENTITLED "SO YOU MAY HEAR" COMES COMPLETE WITH THESE RADICAL FOAM EARS

I THINK THAT WHEN FARMER BOB SAID "HOLY COW" HE WAS JUST USING A FIGURE OF SPEECH

YOU THINK YOUR DEVOTIONS ARE ROUGH? ... WHEN I WAS A KID WE HAD TO READ THE ENTIRE BEGAT SECTION THREE TIMES PER DAY ... IN KJV ... WHILE WALKING THROUGH A BLIZZARD

ONCE THE PHARAOH'S WIZARDS REALIZED THAT THEY COULD NOT BEAT MOSES, THEY TRIED TO IMPRESS HIM WITH THEIR GIANT STAFF

I WOULDN'T WORRY ABOUT ALL THIS YELLING AND SWEARING IF I WERE YOU ... THEY'LL KNOW THAT WE'RE CHRISTIANS BY OUR BUMPER STICKERS

NEAR AS I CAN TELL YOU'VE BEEN SMITTEN ... BEST THING FOR YOU IS TO REPENT AND PRAY TWICE AND THEN CALL ME IN THE MORNING

GENESIS 4:1-15

WELL, ABEL, MY SACRIFICE OF VEGETABLES ISN'T QUITE AS NICE AS YOUR SACRIFICE OF MEAT, BUT AT LEAST I CARED ENOUGH TO SACRIFICE THE FATTED CARROT

MALACHI 3:10

WHEN GOD OPENS THE FLOODGATES OF HEAVEN I PLAN TO BE PREPARED

MY OWNER JUST INFORMED ME THAT I AM NO LONGER HIS BEST FRIEND ... SEEMS HE'S MET SOME CHAP BY THE NAME OF "GOD"

WHILE THE CHOIR IS ON VACATION WE'LL BE SHOWING VIDEOS OF THEIR BEST-LOVED ANTHEMS

GOLIATH NEVER THOUGHT IT WAS FAIR WHEN HE LOST HIS TITLE AS UNDISPUTED CHAMPION OF RECESS DODGEBALL TO SOME KID USING A SLINGSHOT

JUST LOOK AT THIS MESS, ADAM ... WHY DO YOU ALWAYS HAVE TO TRACK MUD ALL OVER CREATION?

OK OK, I'LL ADMIT IT ... I SHOULD HAVE ASKED FOR DIRECTIONS

WE HAVEN'T ACTUALLY FIGURED A WAY FOR OUR "ONLINE PRAYERS" WEBSITE TO GET PRAYERS TO GOD ... WE JUST FIGURE THAT HE'LL SEE PEOPLE TYPING THEM IN

HONESTLY, JESUS, YOU GIVE ME 5 PIES AND 2 TURKEYS AND EXPECT ME TO COOK FOR THE 5,000 GUESTS YOU'VE INVITED?!?

MATTHEW 14:14-21

THE ISRAELITES HATED WAKING UP AFTER A BIG MANNA STORM ONLY TO FIND THAT THEY HAD TO SCRAPE OFF THEIR CAMELS

GENESIS 6-8

THANK YOU, JESUS, FOR ALL THE WONDERFUL FOOD YOU'VE SET BEFORE US ... AMEN

I'M CASSIUS CASSIUM AND I'M COUNTING DOWN THE TOP 40 PSALMS

WITH A SHUDDER OF HORROR JOHN REALIZED THAT HE HAD FORGOTTEN WHERE HE HAD PARKED HIS CAMEL

LORD, I KNOW THE HOLY SPIRIT INSTRUCTS US IN YOUR WORD ... BUT I COULD USE SOME HELP IN MATH HERE TOO

NEXT COMMANDMENT, THOU SHALT NOT KULL ... WAIT A MINUTE ... THAT'S A CHISEL ERROR

CHECK OUT THE FLOOD LIGHTS NOAH ... I'M NOT SURE WHAT THEY DO BUT THEY WERE ON SALE

IF YOU DON'T REGISTER CAT.COM NOW YOU'LL LOSE IT

I'D LIKE TO PRAY TO JESUS ABOUT MY CRIPPLED LEGS BUT I AM AFRAID OF THAT "TAKE UP THY BED AND WALK PART"

YOU SHOULD ALWAYS WEAR CLEAN LEAVES BECAUSE YOU NEVER KNOW WHEN YOU ARE GOING TO GET IN AN ACCIDENT

EWWWWWW

HEY HONEY, MY BEST FRIEND IS HERE AND HE SAYS I HAVE TO DROP EVERYTHING AND GO FISHING

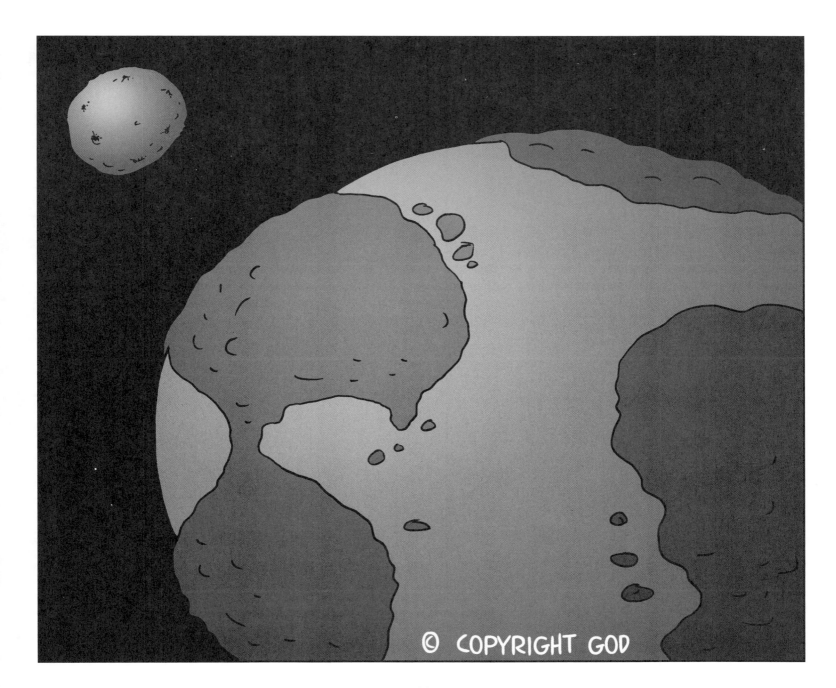

AFTER RETURNING FROM VACATION ED LEARNED A FEW LESSONS:
1. THERE HAD BEEN SOME PLAGUES IN EGYPT
2. THE LOCUST ICE-CUBE GAG WAS NO LONGER FUNNY
3. THE PHARAOH DID NOT HAVE A SENSE OF HUMOR

HOW LONG MUST WE SEARCH FOR THIS "LAND OF PIZZA & SODA" OF WHICH YOU SPEAK? ... MY MOM WILL HAVE DINNER READY SOON

DON'T WORRY, I'M ALRIGHT

I CAN'T WAIT TO SEE MY PARENTS AT THE PEARLY GATES

MATTHEW 14-24-33

PETER, NOT NEEDING A BOARD, COULD SURF ANYTIME THERE WERE
TASTY WAVES

MATT IS WRITING IN TONGUES

LUKE 19-1-10

HEY, I FOUND HIM

BEING AS WE ALL, LIKE SHEEP, HAVE GONE ASTRAY, IT MADE SENSE TO BRING SPORT THE SHEEPDOG HERE ABOARD

WHILE I DO AGREE THAT YOUR IDEA IS QUITE INNOVATIVE I JUST DON'T THINK THAT THE CHURCH IS READY FOR A CARNIVAL APPROACH TO BAPTISM

WOW, ANOTHER ONE OF THE SPIRITUAL GIFTS ... YOU GUYS ROCK

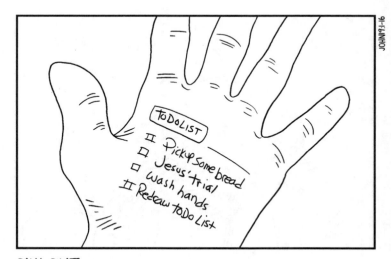

PALM PILATE

113

DANIEL 6

HEY DANIEL, REMEMBER THAT TIME THAT THOSE GUYS THREW YOU IN OUR DEN AND EXPECTED US TO EAT YOU, BUT THEN WE DIDN'T? ... THAT WAS GREAT

OH YEAH, THEY MAKE THIS STUFF UP AND THEN CLAIM THAT THEY EVOLVED FROM US ... I'M SO SURE

ECCLESIASTES 3:1-8

LESSEE ... A TIME TO KILL, A TIME TO HEAL ... UMMM ... A TIME TO RUN AROUND?, TOO BORING ... A TIME FOR HERDING SHEEP?, NO ... SUPPER TIME? ...

I'M SORRY LINDA, "BECAUSE I'M SOOOO CUTE" IS NOT THE ANSWER TO THE BIG QUESTION ... ON TO TOM, WHAT DID YOU HAVE FOR "WHY SHOULD YOU GET INTO HEAVEN?"

YIKES ... I DON'T SUPPOSE YOU LOOKED AT THE "SACRIFICED ON" DATE DID YOU?

DO YOU REALLY NEED ME FOR ME TO EXPLAIN TO YOU WHY I'M RETURNING THIS OUTFIT?

WHAT DO YOU MEAN I SHOULD TRY SHOPPING SOMEWHERE ELSE FOR A CHANGE?

GENESIS 3

YOUR SALT SCULPTURE TITLED "NO LOOKING BACK" IS MAGNIFICENT MR. LOT... TELL US, IS THERE ANY SIGNIFICANCE BEHIND IT?

GENESIS 19:1-29

THEY SAY THAT FAITH CAN MOVE MOUNTAINS ... HOW MUCH FAITH YA GOT?

TODAY'S READING IS MATTHEW 10:30 ... "BUT THE VERY HAIRS OF YOUR HEAD ARE ALL ... ER ... NUMBERED"

IF GOD REALLY LOVES US WHY WOULD HE ALLOW SIN ... AND, WHILE WE'RE ON THE SUBJECT, SLOW MODEMS?

HAPPY VALENTINE'S DAY

HERE YOU ARE, PASTOR BOND, YOUR INSTA VERSE QUOTE 2000 SATELLITE WATCH ... AND SHOULD THINGS GO WRONG OUT THERE, THIS BIBLE CONTAINS A CLEVER DEACON DISGUISE

EXODUS 20:1-21

WE ARE GOING TO FOCUS THE SERMON AGAIN THIS WEEK ON THE MOST IMPORTANT COMMANDMENT ... THOU SHALT NOT KILL

I KNEW IT ... BIBLE CLIFF NOTES

LUKE 2:1-16

LITTLE DID THE SHEPHERDS KNOW WHAT WAS GOING ON WHILE THEY WERE VISITING BABY JESUS IN BETHLEHEM

FROSTY THE SNOWMAN'S MINISTRY WAS SUCCESSFUL UNTIL HE ACCEPTED A CALL TO LOUISIANA

LUKE 11:33

I TOLD YOU ... "HIDE IT UNDER A BUSHEL, NO!!"

HE'S GETTING CRANKY AGAIN ... STAY HIDDEN UNTIL HE COMES OVER AND THEN WE'LL ALL JUMP HIM

JUST ONE DOLLAR ... LOOKS LIKE IT'S TIME FOR THE SERMON ON TITHING AGAIN

OH SURE, WHEN THEY CALLED ME "FATTED CALF" YOU MOCKED ME,
BUT NOW THAT THEY CALL ME THE "PARTY ANIMAL", YOU EXPECT
ME TO LET YOU HANG WITH ME

EXODUS 16

GARY'S SHAPING MANNA-TURKEY, I'M SHAPING MANNA-CHEESE AND
WE'RE STILL LOOKING FOR A GOOD MANNA-BREAD GUY

THOU
SHALT
YIELD

GENESIS 22:15-18

WHAT YOU THOUGHT WAS A BEACH IS ACTUALLY MY DESCENDANTS ...
YOU'LL MEET THE REST OF THEM TONIGHT AFTER DARK

I'M JONAH, I SINNED AGAINST GOD ... WHAT ARE YOU IN FOR?

WHAT I DON'T GET IS ... IF WE PRAYED FOR US TO GET THE MOUSE, WHY WOULDN'T GOD ANSWER OUR PRAYERS?

DOES THIS MEAN THAT YOU AREN'T GOING THE EXTRA MILE?

AS A PROPHET I KNOW THAT I AM GOING TO GET THE JOB ... I WOULDN'T LOOK VERY CONFIDENT IF I DRESSED UP AND SHAVED NOW WOULD I?

BEEP BEEP BEEP BEEP BEEP

THE AD SAID "HOUSE IN SODOM, A FIXER-UPPER" ... I DIDN'T THINK "FIXER-UPPER" MEANT THE CITY

THEY FALL FOR THIS EVERY TIME

HEY BUDDY ... LESS SINGIN', MORE TRUMPETIN'

SAYS HERE THAT OUR SODOM & GOMORRAH IS RATED THE WORST PLACE TO LIVE BASED ON ITS EXCESSIVE DEBAUCHERY ... I WISH SOMEONE WOULD DO SOMETHING ABOUT THAT

GENESIS 19:1-29

STOP ACTING SILLY, JACOB ... YOU KNOW PERFECTLY WELL THAT I ASKED IF YOU KNEW WHERE YOUR BROTHER ESAU WAS

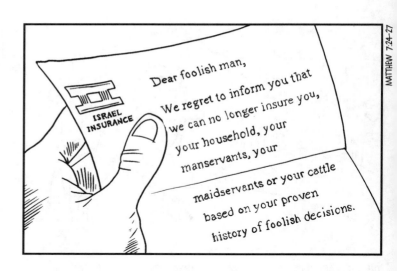

MATTHEW 7:24-27

ISRAEL INSURANCE

Dear foolish man,

We regret to inform you that we can no longer insure you, your household, your manservants, your maidservants or your cattle based on your proven history of foolish decisions.

MATTHEW 10:29-31

PLEASE TRIM NUMBERED HAIRS 1,043 - 3,690 AND 101,972 - 113,010

MENS

HURRY UP IN THERE ... I CAN ONLY KEEP THEM IN SILENT PRAYER FOR SO LONG

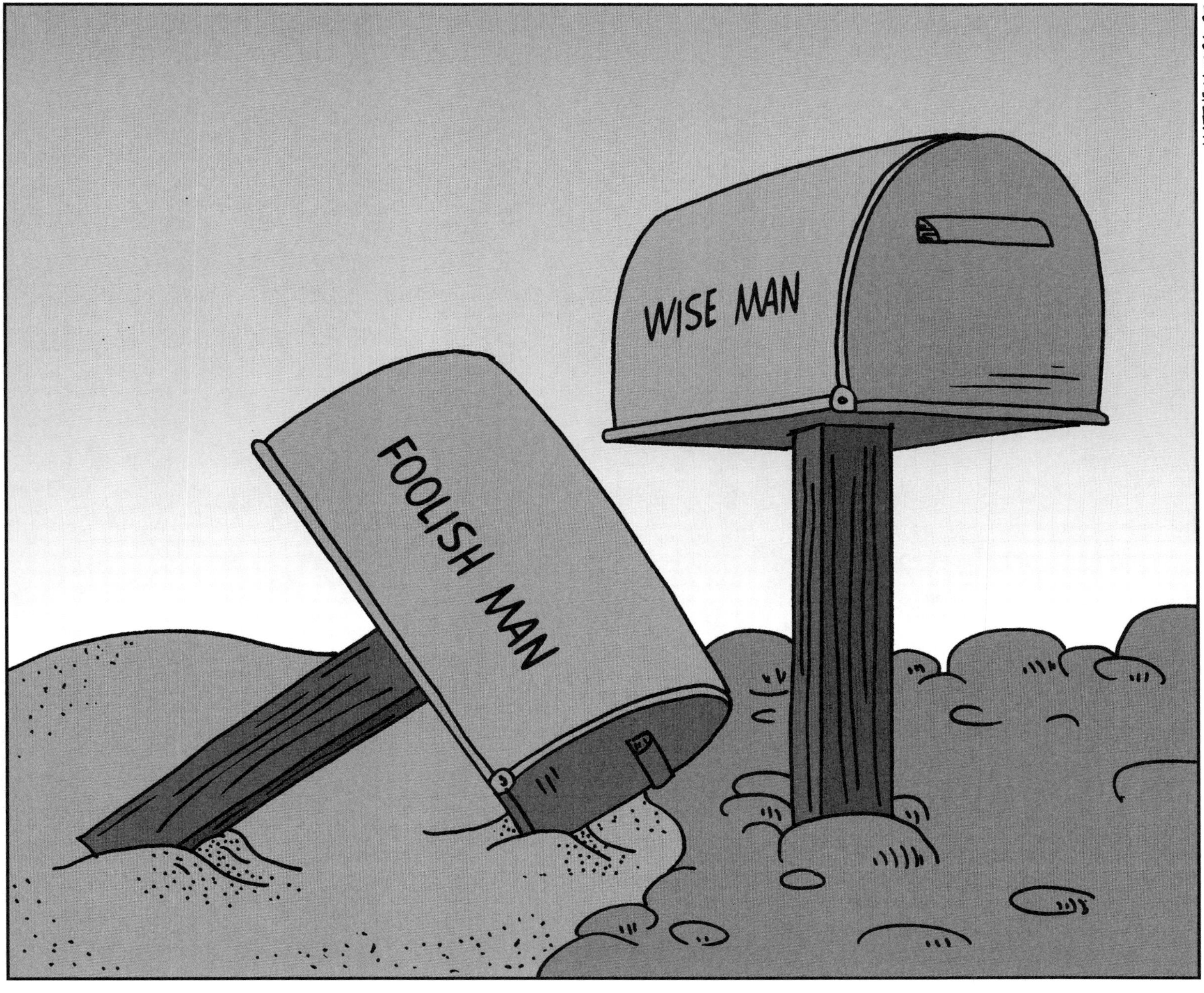

MATTHEW 7:24–27

REVEREND FUN ... ONLINE
HTTP://WWW.REVERENDFUN.COM

The Reverend Fun website features new cartoons every weekday. The site also has years worth of searchable "artchives", updates, merchandise, information about getting and using cartoons in your publications, as well as features and contests. Stop by and see what is happening today.

USING REVEREND FUN CARTOONS
HTTP://WWW.REVERENDFUN.COM/NEEDY/

If you are interested in using Reverend Fun cartoons, please stop by the website to find out more about permissions, credit, and royalties. The site has information about the rules involved in using Reverend Fun as well as tips for getting the cartoons from the site to your bulletin, newsletter, etc...

INTERESTED IN REVEREND FUN GOODIES?
HTTP://WWW.REVERENDFUN.COM/GOODIES/

Looking for that perfect gift? Do you want Reverend Fun paraphernalia to put all over your office? Good for you! Stop by the website and see what is currently available ... and enjoy.